Thank you for choosing
"Simple Succulents and Flowers Coloring: Large Print Color
by Color Me Bright Publishing!

WOULD YOU LIKE A
FREE
PRINTABLE GIFT?

SCAN ME

OR GO TO
http://bit.ly/ColorMeBright

COLOR ME BRIGHT *Publishing*

**YOUR FEEDBACK MEANS
A LOT TO US!**

**Please let us know how we are doing
by leaving us a review on Amazon.**

THIS BOOK BELONGS TO

Caroline Darwin

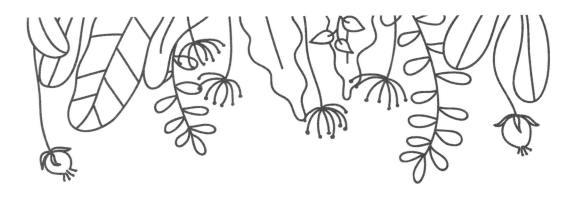

COLOR TEST

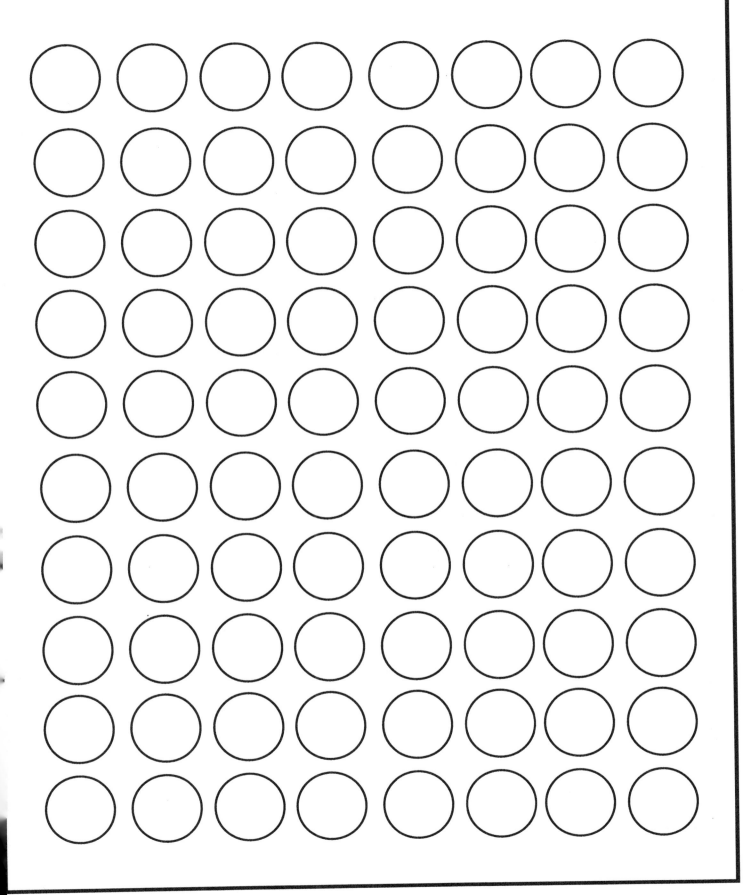

COLOR TEST

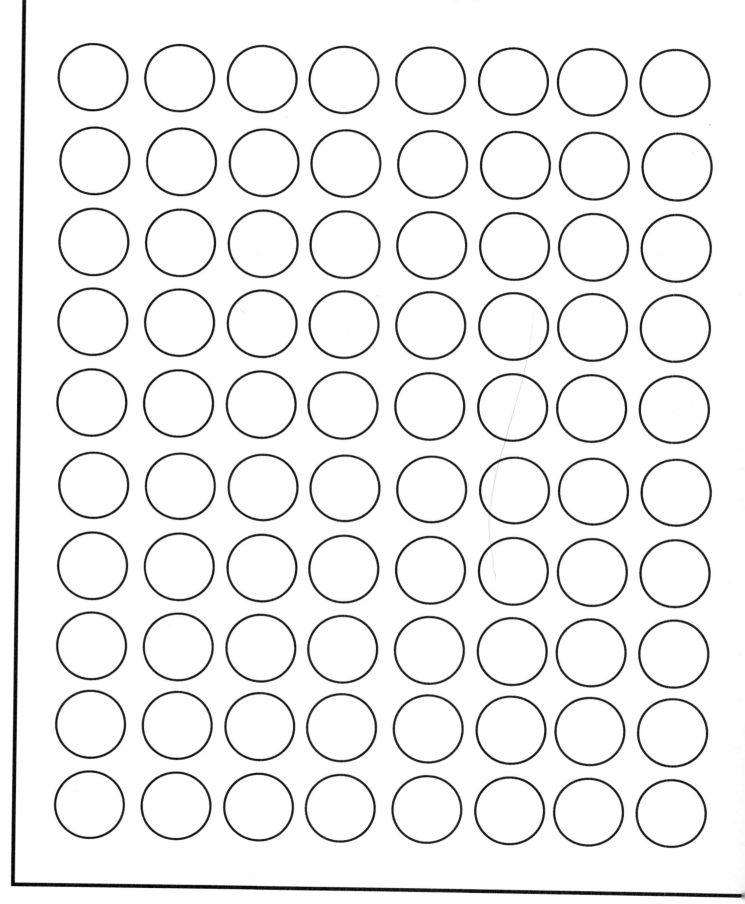

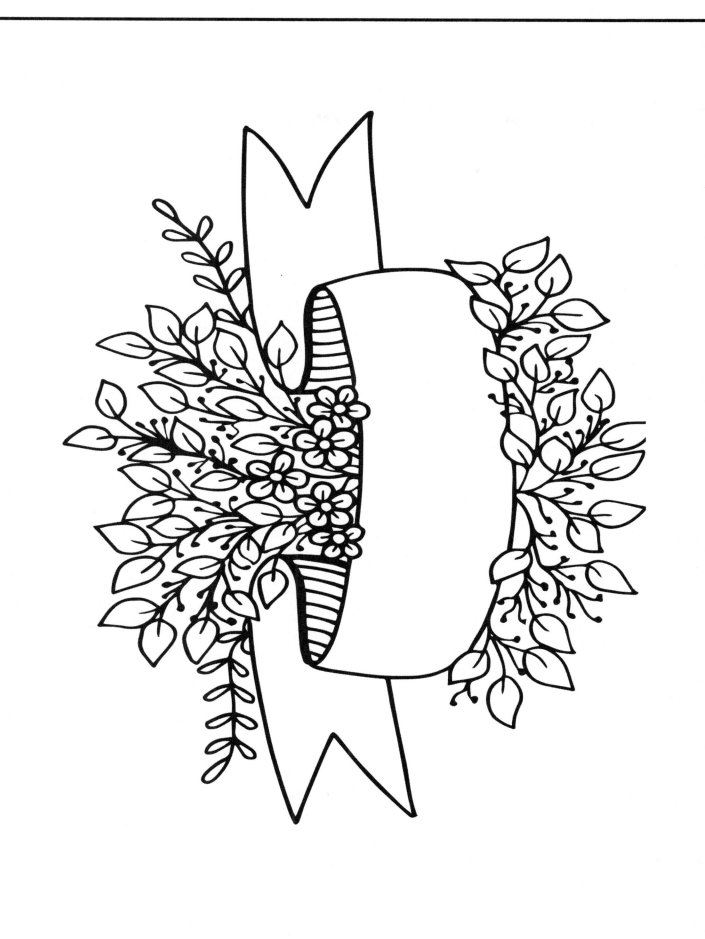

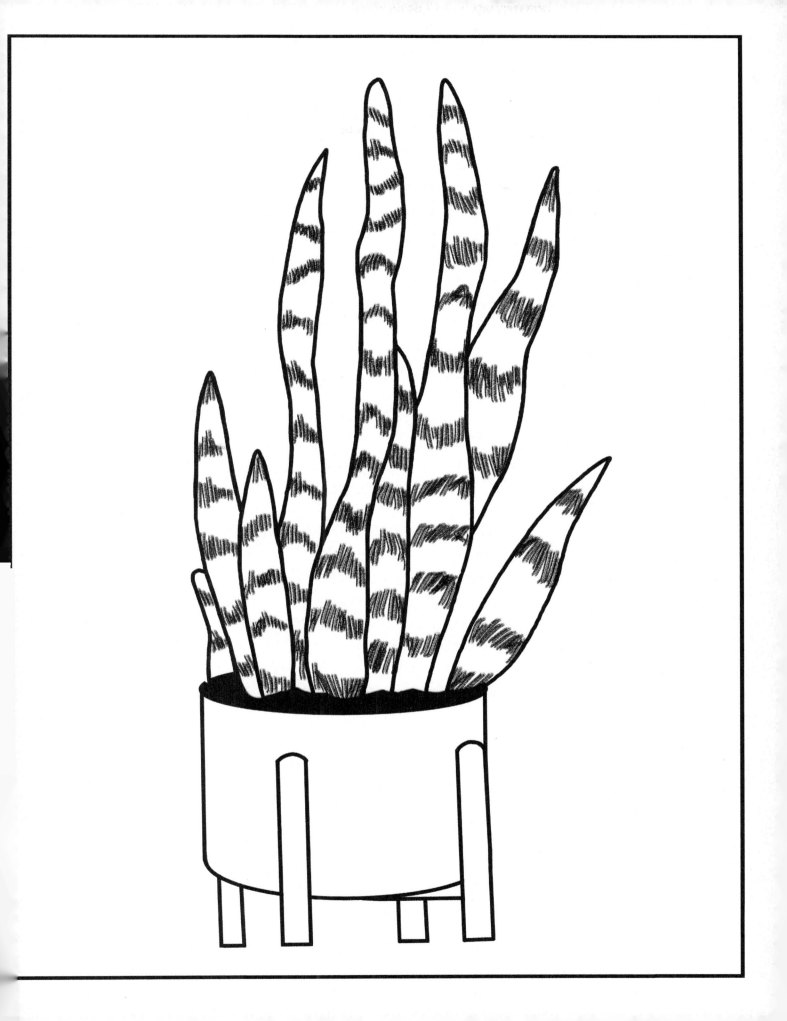

Printed in Great Britain
by Amazon